The Use of Evil

By Annie Besant

Copyright © 2021 Lamp of Trismegistus. All rights reserved. No part of this publication may be reproduced or transmitted in any form or by any means, electronic or mechanical, including photocopying, recording, or by any information storage and retrieval system, without permission in writing from Lamp of Trismegistus. Reviewers may quote brief passages.

ISBN: 978-1-63118-532-8

Esoteric Classics

Other Books in this Series and Related Titles

Aurora of the Philosophers by Paracelsus (978-1-63118-507-6)

Clairvoyance and Psychic Abilities by A Besant &c (978-1-63118-403-1)

The Feminine Occult by various authors (978-1-63118-711-7)

Rosicrucian Rules, Secret Signs, Codes and Symbols by various (978-1-63118-488-8)

An Outline of Theosophy by C W Leadbeater (978-1-63118-452-9)

Paracelsus, the Four Elements and Their Spirits by M P Hall (978-1-63118-400-0)

The Stone of the Philosophers by A E Waite (978-1-63118-509-0)

Essays on the Esoteric Tradition of Karma by A Besant &c (978-1-63118-426-0)

The Rosicrucian Chemical Marriage by Christian Rosenkreuz (978-1-63118-458-1)

The Alchemical Catechism of Paracelsus by Paracelsus (978-1-63118-513-7)

Alchemy in the Nineteenth Century by Helena P Blavatsky (978-1-63118-446-8)

Qabbalistic Teachings and the Tree of Life by M P Hall (978-1-63118-482-6)

The Devil in Love by Jacques Cazotte (978–1–63118–499–4)

Fortune-Telling with Dice by Astra Cielo (978-1-63118-466-6)

History, Analysis and Secret Tradition of the Tarot by Hall &c (978-1-63118-445-1)

Crystal Vision Through Crystal Gazing by Frater Achad (978-1-63118-455-0)

The Golden Verses of Pythagoras: Five Translations (978-1-63118-479-6)

Arcane Formulas or Mental Alchemy by W W Atkinson (978-1-63118-459-8)

The Machinery of the Mind by Dion Fortune (978-1-63118-451-2)

The A E Waite Reader: A Selection of Occult Essays (978-1-63118-515-1)

The Leadbeater Reader: A Selection of Occult Essays (978-1-63118-483-3)

Audio versions are also available on Audible, Amazon and Apple

Other Books in this Series and Related Titles

On the Cave of the Nymphs in the Odyssey by Thomas Taylor (978-1-63118-505-2)

Occult Symbolism of Animals, Insects, Reptiles, Fish & Birds (978-1-63118-420-8)

The Poem of Hashish by A Crowley & C Baudelaire (978-1-63118-484-0)

Brothers & Builders by Joseph Fort Newton (978-1-63118-506-9)

The Kabbalah of Masonry & Related Writings by E Levi &c (978-1-63118-453-6)

A Collection of Fiction and Essays by Occult Writers on Supernatural and Metaphysical Subjects by various (978–1–63118–510–6)

The Sepher Yetzirah and the Qabalah by M P Hall (978-1-63118-481-9)

Cloud Upon the Sanctuary by Waite & K Eckartshausen (978-1-63118-438-3)

The Hymns of Hermes by G R S Mead (978-1-63118-405-5)

The Secrets of Enoch by Enoch (978-1-63118-449-9)

Masonic and Rosicrucian History by M P Hall & H Voorhis (978-1-63118-486-4)

The Sword of Welleran and Other Stories by Lord Dunsany (978-1-63118-501-4)

The Eleusinian Mysteries and Rites by Dudley Wright (978–1–63118–530–4)

Gnosis of the Mind by G. R. S. Mead (978-1-63118-408-6)

The First and Second Gospels of the Infancy of Jesus Christ (978-1-63118-415-4)

The Life of Pythagoras by Porphyry (978-1-63118-512-0)

Freemasonry & Catholicism by Max Heindel (978-1-63118-508-3)

Rosicrucians and Speculative Masonry in the Seventeenth Century (978-1-63118-489-5)

The Influence of Pythagoras on Freemasonry and Other Essays (978-1-63118-404-8)

The Path of Light: A Manual of Maha-Yana Buddhism (978-1-63118-471-0)

Tao Te Ching & Commentary by Lao Tzu & C Johnston (978-1-63118-495-6)

Audio versions are also available on Audible, Amazon and Apple

Table of Contents

Introduction…7

The Use of Evil…9

INTRODUCTION

The word "esoteric" can be difficult to define. Esotericism in general can be seen less as a system of beliefs and more as a category, which encompasses numerous, different systems of beliefs. It's a bit of juxtaposition, since the word "esoteric" indicates something that few people know about, while the term itself broadly covers numerous philosophies, practices, areas of study and belief systems.

In a greater sense, Esotericism acts as a storehouse for secret knowledge, which is often considered ancient (by *tradition, if not by fact),* passed down from generation to generation, in private. At various times in history, simply possessing the knowledge of some of these subjects, was considered illegal and a jailable offence, if discovered. This usually included such general topics as Alchemy, Pharmacology, Qabalah, Hermeticism, Occultism, Ceremonial Magic, Astrology, Divination, Rosicrucianism and so on. Collectively, these areas of study were often referred to as the esoteric sciences.

Sometimes, the outer garment of a subject isn't esoteric, while what is hidden beneath it, is. As an example, Freemasonry isn't necessarily esoteric by nature (at *least not anymore),* but certain signs, passwords and handshakes given to the candidate during their initiation, are in fact, esoteric, in the sense that they are hidden from the general public.

Today, in the twenty-first century, such topics are readily available at bookstores across the country, and numerous mainsteam publishers offer beginners guides and coffee-table volumes on many of these subjects, intended for mass appeal. Books like *"The Secret"* have turned previously arcane topics into household knowledge. All that being the case, however, it isn't to say that there still aren't buried secrets to uncover, ancient wisdom being ignored and forgotten mysteries to be explored. In fact, it is often that we are only able to further our own studies by standing on the shoulders of these disappearing giants.

Lamp of Trismegistus is doing its part to help preserve humanity's esoteric history by making some of these classics available to those students who are seeking to unearth the knowledge of these ancient colossi.

So, be sure to check other titles from our *Esoteric Classics* series, as well as our *Occult Fiction, Theosophical Classics, Foundations of Freemasonry Series, Supernatural Fiction, Paranormal Research Series, Studies in Buddhism* and our *Christian Apocrypha Series*. You can also download the audio versions of most of these titles from Amazon, Apple or Audible, for learning on the go.

THE USE OF EVIL

My Brothers:

I am to speak to you this evening on a problem which has tasked the intellect of man for thousands and thousands of years and which is still discussed today, as though it had never been considered before, with as much energy and eagerness and with as much interest. That it remains unsolved still is shown by the continuance of the discussion and by this unwearied turning to it of the mind of man. Man seems instinctively to imagine that this problem is one which would teach lessons of value and importance, if it could be understood, and that behind the "Mystery of Evil" there is hidden some priceless truth.

I do not pretend that I am going to solve this immemorial problem, but I hope to lay before you certain considerations which may throw light upon it, if you apply yourselves to thinking over them. And in order that you may carry them more easily in your minds I divide the subject under four heads:

1. The Origin of Evil.

2. The Relativity of Evil.

3. The Use of Evil.

4. The Ending of Evil.

Under these four heads I hope to show you that evil is a necessary part of manifestation, a necessary condition of manifestation, and originates with manifestation. That also it does not exist absolutely, in and by itself, but is relative, relative in that it exists in relations between things and not in the things themselves, and also because it varies with time, with succession of events, and with the progress of the universe. Then I hope to show you the purposes it sub-serves, the uses it fulfills, and lastly how we may escape from it, how we may, by the use of evil, break the bonds that tie us to the wheel of birth and death; how although living in the world, we may live in it without generating karma, and so, to use a well- known phrase, may burn up karma in the fire of Knowledge. Following these divisions under which I shall arrange the details, I may be able to give to your minds, the minds of the rising and educated youth of India, ideas that may be worthy of your consideration, in order that you may not simply listen for an hour, but taking them at leisure, may have materials to work upon after you have left this hall.

Now let us consider the Origin of Evil. Realize, to begin with, that no universe can come into manifestation at all, that no manifestation can occur, that no multiplicity can become, that no diversity can appear, unless there be limitation. That is the first point that I wish to make clear to your minds. The one existence, spoken of sometimes as Brahman, that existence is absolute and undivided; no attributes are there, no qualities are there. There is unity, no diversity; there is unity, no multiplicity. It is "the One without a second". So that, when for a moment you try even to think this Existence, in the very thinking by which you must separate yourself from It, by which you as a mind endeavor to consider something which is thought of and is not the thinker, by that very effort of thought you introduce duality into that which you are trying to realize as unity; and when there is separation between the thinker and thought, which is implied in the effort, there is diversity — not Brahman as One in whom there is no duality, in whom there is no separated Being, in whom there is neither thinker nor thought. Thought implies perception and an object of perception; but Brahman is absolute unity, absolute identity. We speak of thought where thought cannot exist. It is unconditioned, therefore unintelligible; unconditioned, therefore without limitation. And therefore, truly is it written, THAT is neither conscious nor unconscious — albeit there is some deeper essence which, when conditioned, becomes consciousness, because consciousness implies duality, consciousness implies something which is conscious, and something of which it is conscious. That is, at least duality is implied the very moment the word consciousness is used, so that in that absolute unity, where there is identity and not diversity, where there is but the secondless ONE, there is no possibility of thinking, because there is absence of conditions, there is absence of limitation. But the very moment the universe has, as it were, to come into being, then there must be conditions, there must be limitation. Limitation is a condition of manifestation, for the very moment you arrive at the point of manifestation, a circumference must be drawn from the central point, the circle of a universe; without that, thought is lost in the absolute one-ness, the identity. Within that circle thought may be exercised, and the very word 'manifestation' implies at once this limitation.

Manifestation, by a law of mind, at once implies its antithesis, the absence of manifestation. To anything which you may think, comes the opposite, for the opposite is implied in the very act of defining. 'A' implies 'not-A'. Therefore we are compelled to formulate 'absence of manifestation', and yet cannot truly be said to think it. But as I have just said, manifestation must imply limitation. There is limitation in the very existence of a universe; it is conditioned, and as soon as you think of the matter you at once begin to understand that a universe implies limitation, and that only by a process of limitation can a universe come into being; conditions self-imposed within the Infinite One-ness that can be recognized as the boundary that limits thought. Well, when that is thought and understood, the next step is very simple. Having diversity, having limitation, there is at once imperfection implied. The perfect is unlimited; the limited, imperfect. So imperfection must be the result of limitation. In the totality you may find perfection; in the whole, but not in the parts. The very moment you have parts, multiplicity, various bodies, each body separately considered is imperfect, because it is less than the whole. The very fact that it is a part proves that it is imperfect; a fragment cannot be perfect; only the whole can have perfection predicated of it. So that we have here the second step. The first is the fact of manifestation implying limitation, and thus limitation making a diversity of objects; the second is that separate bodies must be imperfect, in that each is less than the whole of which only perfection can be declared.

Notice now the links of the argument. Notice that the very fact of a universe implies this imperfection; that if you object to imperfection, you must object to manifestation. If you object to limitation, you must object to there being anything which can be thought of, of which consciousness can be predicated, anything save that absolute unity utterly incomprehensible to thought. So that we have this solid ground to start from that the existence itself of the universe by the very fact of limitation, implies imperfection in the limited and that every object being necessarily limited, is also necessarily imperfect, being less than the whole. Now when that is realized, you have your origin of imperfection, of what is called evil. Thus imperfection is co-eternal with the universe. Limited, imperfection is a necessary condition, so that whenever there comes a universe into existence, imperfection must come into existence at the same time. The fact of manifestation is the origin of imperfection.

But when we go on to deal with what is called evil, we find something more in our thoughts than this necessary imperfection of separated bodies; although the essence of imperfection is in the very existence of the universe, that which we call evil lies in the degree of imperfection, and in its relation to the rest. But in the very words 'good and evil' relativity is fundamentally implied, the 'pairs of opposites' necessary to thought; the word 'good' is not fairly to be predicated of any thing until the idea of evil is recognized — the 'not-good'; for good and evil are correlative terms, and the one can only be distinguished as being the opposite of the other, which is implicitly present in the mind at the same time. It is a fundamental law of mind that thought must work by difference, discriminating the difference, technically, between 'A' and 'not-

A'; 'A' representing the individual thing which is thought of, and 'not-A' everything else which is excluded from that individual thing; so that if you say 'good' you separate the good from that from which it is distinguished — the 'not-good'; and without this separation no idea of good can be present in the mind, for we realize 'good' only by contrast with that which is 'not good' and which is distinguished from it. In the absence of that distinguishment there would be nothing which we could call 'good'. 'Good' and 'not good', then, are a pair of opposites. And one is only possible by the existence of the other. Similarly you may take another pair of opposites. Compare light with darkness. Light would have no meaning to you in thought if it were not for darkness or not-light. Light is only cognizable by thought because of not-light. Light-giving bodies can be recognized in thought, because all bodies do not give light; and this is so much the case that the presence of non-light giving bodies is necessary for realization of light. Astronomers tell us, startling as seems the statement, that the depths of space are dark, not light, although they are full of the vibrations of the ether which on the earth we recognize as light. Why? Because there are vast spaces of the mighty universe where there are no light-reflecting bodies, themselves non-luminous; and in the absence of these dark ones light cannot be thrown back, reflected; hence space which is full of the vibrations of ether is absolutely dark, because of the absence of those bodies which are the reflectors of light, themselves being dark.

Take still further an extension of the same thought. Evil does not exist in and by itself, as we may judge from the phenomena around us; evil, like good, lies in the relationship between one thing and another; it is relative, not absolute. What we speak of as evil in one place may be not evil in another; for evolution implies this changing character, and what is good at one stage may be evil at another. Presently I will take certain things which we say are evil, and show you that the evil does not reside in the things, but in the relationships between them and certain other things, and that it is in the relationship alone that what we call evil resides. Let me take an illustration to show you what I mean. You may have a violently vibrating body, vibrating without touching any other body, vibrating inwards and outwards, which would do no harm, which would cause no pain, and the result of that active motion of the body would not be anything which you would recognize as evil. But place in contact with that violently vibrating body another body, and it will produce what we call a pleasure or a pain — that is if the second body has got the power of response, the power of answering to that which is outside, and of feeling the vibration to which it answers. By coming into contact with the body which is violently vibrating, and by receiving the blow, what we call the sensation of pain might arise. Now pain is regarded as part of the evil of the universe; pain is regarded as one of those things which are the results of what is called evil. But as a matter of fact, pain is the result of contact between two things which separately are innocuous, and arises from the inter-relation of those things which in their separate aspects are not individually pain-producing, but only imperfect, each by itself. When coming into relation with each other, they, as it were, work against each other; then there comes out what we regard as evil, and the nature of the result will depend upon the relation between the two, not even upon the inherent imperfections of each that I spoke of, but on their relations to each other.

Now that leads me to point out to you that as evolution proceeds, that which we call evil must necessarily be developed more and more. As evolution proceeds, the result of the evolution is to bring into conscious existence higher and higher types of organizations, higher and higher types of living things, which enter into more and more complicated relationships with others which surround them, and in these organizations there is developed more and more of this power of response. There is developed also the memory of response; there is developed not only memory, but the power of placing things side by side, that is of comparison, and then of considering the results of the comparison, and drawing therefrom volitions. And then there is the experience gradually gathered which illumines the developing consciousness, enables it to recognize certain things as things found to be against progress, to be against the higher evolution, certain things which retard evolution, certain things which check it, which tend to bring about disintegration instead of higher integration. Now what means evolution? It is merely the building together of higher and more complicated organizations which express with ever greater and greater perfection the Life that is Divine, the Life that in the universe is seeking manifestation. When we speak of manifestations as higher or lower, we really mean that they express more or less of the Divine. We call them higher and lower merely as they manifest qualities which tend towards the lessening of separateness and the developing of unity, that is which lead away from the pole of matter and lead towards the pole of

Spirit. The grosser side of manifestation of the One Life is that which we describe as matter. Now there are two poles in manifestation: the form-side, or that of matter, on the one hand, and the life-side, or that of Spirit, on the other. They are the two opposite aspects of the one Eternal Life, and the process of evolution consists in that life in its dual aspects going out-wards to cause diversity, and when the limit of diversity is reached, drawing inwards to reintegrate the diverse separated units into a mighty and enriched unity. The outward-going life seeks diversity and may be said therefore to tend to the pole of matter; the inward-going life seeks unity, and may be said therefore to tend to the pole of Spirit. Here is a truth that the thoughtful should ponder over. If we take good to mean all that is working in harmony with the Great Law, and evil to mean all that is working against it, then qualities now regarded, and rightly regarded, as evil — selfishness, desire for material gain, etc. — would have been good during the 'descent into matter', as only by these could diversity be obtained. Whereas now they are evil as retarding the process of integration, as checking the inward-flowing tide of life towards the pole of Spirit. Thus again we realize the relativity of evil, and understand that a quality which at one time was good, as sub-serving the progress of the universe, becomes evil when it should have been left behind in the sweep of evolution, and when, persisting into a stage higher than that to which it belonged, it retards the progress which once it had accelerated.

Evolution, on its returning path, is unfolding the life-side of nature, and is making, as it were, matter more and more plastic, more and more delicate, more and more complicated in its organization, until by its very complexity its equilibrium is so unstable that it takes very easily shapes of various kinds under impulses from within and becomes a mere graceful garment in which life is expressed, until, finally, matter is nothing more than the subtle form which expresses life by limiting it, and it changes form with every impulse from the life, and takes on new shapes with the different impulses of the outgoing and in- coming life; and this is evolution. When man begins to understand what evolution means, he then regards everything which helps towards evolution as being on the lines of harmony with the purposes of the universe, and therefore with being now on the side of greater and greater integration, of the building together of a complicated unity. Then he names 'good' all that works in that direction, and calls 'evil' all the tendencies which persist from the stage of evolution in which greater diversity was sought. Realizing that evolution is now the process of building together the separated objects into a perfect unity, he calls 'good' everything which tends directly to harmony, which tends towards aggregation, which tends towards the unfolding of the higher unity, which tends towards the expression of the Divine Life, with ever increasing and increasing perfection; and he calls 'evil' everything which checks that aggregation, and which introduces the earlier forms into the present and retards the passing on to what is relatively perfect and relatively higher.

Now suppose we carried that thought out, what would we find? We should find that, that which, in the past, caused evolution and was not evil, becomes evil when it persists in the evolution of the higher organization and so retards its growth.

For instance: in the mineral kingdom you have minerals and stones hurled about by some volcanic eruption; you see that eruption, with its shivering of certain bodies, with its tremendous evolution of gases, accompanied by explosions, and then with the rebound of the separate materials making a desert where before was a fertile plain, and you say: "See, this is evil". Yet wiser minds, on the contrary, regard it as part of the regenerative processes of nature, by which, by disintegration and collision, new combinations are rendered possible, the face of the earth is changed, mountain ranges are thrown up, rivers and channels are created, and by means of this violent destructive agency, new continents are built, homes for higher forms of life are rendered possible in the course of the evolution. Let us pause for a moment and contemplate the way in which a continent is built. Let us watch the tremendous action of those volcanic forces, and at one place see a mountain range flung up; then let us watch the formation of mighty glaciers, great masses of ice, and see them presently begin to grind their way down the mountain-side into the plain which lies below; see their resistless course, plowing out their way, and listen as they go on smashing, grinding, shivering, tossing up masses which fall again rebounding; watch the processes of that world of struggle, of strife, of noise, of disturbance, of difficulty, and see the marshaling of those energies which seem to be working for ruin and for nothing else. But as centuries go on, and still you are watching, you find that where there was a grinding glacier, there is now a new channel, a channel which has been dug out of the mountain-side and through the plains by its giant action, and as you watch you find water collecting in this channel, and gradually, more and more flowing into it, until where there was the destructive action of the ice, there is a great river full of life-giving water; and as the water flows down through the plain vegetation springs up on the banks, and great cities are building, food can be grown for keeping up the life of man, trees are growing luxuriantly, and human homes are seen, and happiness on every side. But what would have been man's lot without that previous evolution? We can see that unless the disturbing agency had had full sway in these earlier growths of life, you would never have had the later; so you cannot call that evil. There is nothing evil in itself, for these are simply destructive and attractive forces at work, and the Being who is the source of all life, the great One, the Lord, is known sometimes as the Destroyer and sometimes as the Regenerator, for until the lower is destroyed the higher cannot be born, and every death is but the lower aspect of a higher birth.

But if we turn to man, to those who have been gradually evolved, those human beings who have begun to reason, who have begun to remember, to compare, and therefore to judge and to understand — when amongst them there appears a disturbing agency, which lies at the root of all the angry passions of man, then man, having evolved to a stage at which the infliction of pain on others is against his evolution towards the Divine Love, we call that infliction of pain a 'crime'. Why, for instance, do we call a murder an evil act? We call it an evil because the murderer is there reverting to a previous stage in evolution which he ought to have outgrown; as a man he should have evolved towards a higher life of harmony, but he is giving way to an inclination which will bring about the retardation of growth, and which at the stage which he has reached is harmful. At the point of evolution he should have reached, he ought to be one of the forces evolving towards the Divine Harmony, and not one of the forces which are retarding that evolution, and rendering it slower of accomplishment.

I am going to deal with the use of this retarding agency. Let us take now a man who begins to understand that in the sphere of thought and action he can place himself either upon the side of progress or upon the side of retardation; who realizes his place in the universe, who realizes the true working of nature, and who may deliberately set himself either on the side of the evolving life, or upon the side of the forces which are retarding evolution, which are holding it back, which are against progress, which are not in harmony with it. Such a man has to choose with which side he shall identify himself. He may choose to identify himself with the side which is progressing on to the Gods, or he may choose to identify himself with the side which is retarding that evolution. His choice is in his own hands. He must realize that if he chooses the side which retards evolution he has chosen destruction, by identifying himself with the disintegrating agency; whereas if he chooses harmony with evolving life, he has chosen continuation, because he has identified himself with that which is the law of progress, and the fact of his identification with that law will give to him the permanence which results from harmony. You may say: Why should identification with the retarding forces lead to destruction? The answer is this: Because the Divine Life, going on and causing evolution, returns to unity, and everything which harmonizes with its mighty course is carried onwards without waste of energy; whereas everything which sets itself against it, and causes friction and retardation, wears itself out by the very friction which it causes. It is one of the laws of motion that a moving body continues to move if not opposed, but if friction is generated by its coming into contact with another body it will gradually come to a standstill; wherever there is friction, there is this expenditure of energy, and this friction transmutes moving energy into another form, such as heat, and the energy is dissipated; continued friction causes the dissipation of the form which is subject to it. It is not that the energy is annihilated; it is not that the energy is destroyed; that cannot be. It is that the form is destroyed, for it comes into contact with that in which the opposite force is manifested. The form perishes, because the opposition breaks it into pieces, or rather, it breaks itself into pieces against the opposing force, but the energy persists, because it is part of one eternal life. But you may say: Why this retarding force? Why should there be in evolution this action of retardation? Why should there be in evolution something which opposes? How can it come? If everything is from the One, how can it develop? First, because the condition of any diversity is the manifestation of the opposing poles of Spirit and matter, of light and darkness, that I spoke of in the beginning; and secondly, because for the development of all positive qualities, it is necessary that they should be exercised against opposition. Without opposition no development is possible; without opposition no growth is possible. All growth and development result from the exercise of energy against something which opposes. Think for a moment, and you will see how true this statement is. You have muscles in your arms; if you want to develop the strength of the muscles; how are you to do it? By exercising them, by stimulating them, not by keeping them still. You know there are some people who practice a particular form of asceticism, who extend the arm and keep it rigid, so that muscular contraction cannot take place. What is the result? After a time, the arm becomes fixed in that position, it becomes rigid, the muscles lose the power of contraction; they are no longer the channels of living energy; in fact, there is stagnation, absence of effort, absence of muscular contraction, of pulling against resistant forces; the result is to throw the arm backwards, as it were, into a lower form of living thing, to which motion as a whole does not belong, and the arm becomes as rigid as a stone or a piece of wood; it has lost the muscular power for want of exercise, because it has remained quiet and stagnant, and therefore the power of motion has disappeared. But if a man wants to develop his muscles, what does he do? He takes a club which has weight, he takes a dumb-bell which has weight, he takes any object which has weight, and then sets muscle against weight and pulls against it, whirls it round, but always puts the muscle against the opposing force in the weight. He lifts it from the ground; and the weight tries to drag him down and he tries to drag it up. The effect of this conflict is the development of muscular energy, the development of force in the muscle. Muscularity is drawn out and developed by working against the opposing weight; it becomes stronger and becomes able to overcome opposing forces, and so the muscle grows and develops the more, the more it is exercised, and becomes more powerful than before. This development arises entirely because it has been used in opposing weight, and by exercise has overcome the opposition; from this it has gathered life and strength, for as the muscle increases its capacity for holding life,

life flows into it, and ever the strength we can draw from the surrounding divine Life is limited only by our capacity to receive and hold.

There is the use of evil. The life that is in you cannot manifest its higher capacities unless you are placed under conditions in which you can develop yourselves by struggling against opposition. Evil is, as it were, the weight opposing the muscle, and as you develop the body by struggling against the opposing external weight, so do you develop the moral character by struggling against evil which is the opposite of every virtue. Every virtue has its opposite evil. Truth and falsehood, courage and cowardice, compassion and hatred, humility and pride. All these things are pairs of opposites. How can you develop truth save by struggling against the false, save by realizing that in the world around you there is falsehood on every side of you? What can you do when you realize the force of this, save contradict it and place yourself in opposition to it, and yourself be true? Never let a false word escape your lips; never let a false thought find habitation in your brain, never let a false action disfigure your conduct, and the result of the recognition of falsehood will be to develop in you the necessary power for truth. As you struggle against the tendency to falseness, there is developed in you the increasing power to be true. Now what is Truth? Truth is Brahman: Truth is life: Truth is the essence of what we call the divine Life; and we reach it by struggling against falsehood, developing as it were, the virtue which is the receptacle of the divine Life, and as you enlarge it and increase it by your struggling against falsehood — as the muscle grows larger by practice against the weight — you are making your character a receptacle for the divine Life, that divine Life which shall flow in, in ever-increasing volume and give you greater power. Thus you are developing those qualities of Truth which, without opposition, you could never have evolved and which, in proportion to the energies evolved by your efforts against falsehood, will purify your nature from falsity, and render true the life which you are developing. So also with every other virtue. Courage is developed in the presence, not in the absence, of an object which you fear. If there were no objects which gave rise to the sensation of fear, then courage could never be evolved. But the presence of these objects that give the sensation of fear increases the experience of the Soul and gradually evolves courage. Have you ever noticed in an infant, that, that which at first was terrifying to it, that which was an object of terror to it when first seen, gradually loses its terrifying quality as it becomes more and more familiar? See how timid a little child is; see how he sees even in a strange face, an object which terrifies him. How shall that child lose that timidity and become brave in the face of men? Not by shutting him up in a room where he will never see anybody. If you keep him in a room where there is no strange face, the child has no fear. Fear is generated by letting him face unknown objects, and presently he begins to understand them, until out of constant experiences fear is eliminated, and strength and courage take its place.

And so I might take virtue after virtue to show that they grow only in the face of opposition, and that in the result of these opposing forces lies the value of this retarding energy: *there* is the value of the evolution of evil which acts as a weight against the effort towards perfection, and thereby develops the strength which checks the desire for these forms which are doomed to destruction; for the men who choose to ally themselves with that which is doomed to destruction must share the fate of those forms they have selected for their own. But the energy which is necessary for evolution towards the condition of perfection would be absent without evil, and the presence of evil in the universe makes it possible for good to grow and for perfection to triumph.

Nor must we forget, as a fundamental use of evil, the evolution of the power to discriminate between good and evil, and thus of volition, of choice. How should we distinguish Truth save by discerning it as different from that which is not true? How should we learn its value if we did not find from experience the destructive effects of falsehood, in man and in society. 'A' is only brought into consciousness by the presence of 'not-A' and the latter is necessary to the definition of the former in the mind. So our mind would remain a blank as regards Truth; we could not realize it, cognize it, define it, save as distinguishing it by its differences from not-Truth. And so with each virtue, with good in its totality. Only by recognition of evil can we know good. And to recognition of evil, experience of evil is necessary.

Useful also is evil as a scourge that drives us to good. For as evil is discordance with the evolving forces of the divine Life in manifestation, it must result in pain. Pain verily *is* discordant vibration. Therefore evil inevitably brings suffering as a result, not by an arbitrary penalty but by an inherent necessity. And suffering gives rise to a feeling of repulsion towards the cause of suffering, and so drives man away from the side of nature which inharmoniously and tumultuously is plunging into disintegration, and carrying with it the personalities who elect to identify themselves therewith. In the mighty stream of divine Life that circles as a universe all men are carried along; but one current whirls downwards all monstrous and disorderly growths, that they may be disintegrated into the rough materials for a new building, while the other current carries onwards all that are molding themselves into orderly expressions, and that by making themselves vehicles of the Law share its permanence as an essential manifestation of the One Reality. I said, when dealing with pain, that I would show you how evil can be got rid of; I also said that I would show you how it was possible that this evil which we see around us and recognize as evil, might gradually lose over us its retarding power as the God in us evolves outwardly and fills us with strength. Remember that the line, along which I have been leading you, will enable you to look with understanding and therefore with absolute charity on all the forms of evil which surround you; you will see in them inevitable imperfections; if you see the human Soul struggling in corruption and in evil, you will not feel anger, nor intolerance, nor hatred, but you will know that this Soul, just because of the evil with which it is struggling, will gradually gain strength and become triumphant over it. So that at last you will understand how the Divine is in everything, in good as in evil, that Sri Krishna is the vice of the gambler as well as the purity of the righteous, and our universe will become full of hope; for you will recognize that the whole is working towards perfection, and that good and evil are the two forces which co-operate to liberate the Soul, the one by drawing it upwards, the other by shattering everything to which it clings and which is not God. But the point to which I wish to lead you is, that as you gradually recognize these facts you will see that the aim of the individual Self is to become perfectly at one with the inward-going stream of divine Life: this is the beginning of understanding, the beginning of the realization of the meaning of the universe, and you will begin to utilize what seems to be evil in order that you may get rid of everything which binds you down to the transitory side of nature, and so take pain as a real helper. Pain is said to be an evil. Pain is not pleasant, but it is not an evil; it is desirable and not undesirable, for it is a condition of gaining perfection, and without it perfection cannot be. And why? For this reason; that development must become conscious, that is, there must be a gradual development of thought within us. But by what process can this be secured? When we go outward towards an object which attracts us we at first seek only satisfaction. But in the external there is no permanent satisfaction; in the external which attracts the deluded Soul of man there is nothing that can give permanent satisfaction to the Soul. The Soul has been compared to a charioteer, standing in the chariot of the body, and using the mind as the reins to curb the horses of the senses; when the galloping horses of the senses carry the soul away to the objects of desire, how shall the Soul learn that these objects are not truly desirable? How shall he lose the desire which goes out to these things which can never satisfy? And how shall he learn to turn inward to the center, and seek for Brahman alone? He can only be led to turn from his desires, when he finds that every thing which is not Brahman passes away, and in the passing away gives pain. You desire the gratification of the senses. How shall that desire be eliminated? Only by discovering that the pleasure they yield is very transitory, that if it is followed too far it brings about disgust and suffering and pain, and that therefore the freedom and the wisdom of man lie in getting rid of the desire for sense-pleasures. If having been attracted by the sensation of taste, because it is pleasant, we find that to gratify it to the utmost brings disgust, then we begin to see that it will be wiser to choose an object which has more permanence than the gratification of taste. Then the root of desire is pulled up, and can send out these lower shoots no more. But you can never convince men that this is so unless they have tried the following of the objects of the lower desires and have found the results which flow from them. Argument would not do it, reasoning would not do it, but when men have had the experience, when men have gratified their taste to the full, when they have become gluttonous, presently they will find that they have made their bodies miserable, their lives one long suffering, that diseases result from the gratification they have experienced, that the gratification brings *pain* as a result; then they will no longer desire to gratify themselves in that way, and the root of desire will be cut away; or rather the process of cutting it away will have begun, for the process is a long one. And that is the only way desire can be finally extirpated. You can only get rid of it by gradually realizing through experience the knowledge that the gratification of all desire which is not going upwards is a womb of pain, and brings forth woe as a child. Nothing but this experience can get rid of desire; not by outward compulsion, but by inward will, must the destruction of desire take place, and this is wrought by pain. Hence is pain, miscalled an evil, one of the greatest blessings bestowed upon man, in order to turn him from the transitory and fix him upon the eternal; for only by pain can he possibly learn, only out of disgust with the world will arise those inward aspirations which shall at last be gratified in the vision of Truth Divine.

Do not misunderstand me, for misunderstanding on this matter is very easy but very dangerous. The stage of the full gratification of desire that I have been speaking of is the stage of the Soul's childhood, ere yet the memory of the Soul, recalling past suffering following on gratification, translates itself as the voice of conscience, and warns the lower nature of the peril of yielding to desire. When once experience has been sufficient to bring about such warning from the Soul then it is madness to disregard it and gratify desire in its despite. Full gratification of desire belongs to the stage where the outer attraction is yielded to without a pause, without a doubt, without a question, and is followed by no regret, by no shame, by no remorse. The rising of any question in the mind as to the propriety or the wisdom of gratifying the desire, shows that the memory of the Soul contains a record of suffering following on similar gratification in the past; otherwise no question could arise. If the man yields, against the warning, the pain of remorse will be added to the pain of satiety, and only thus progressive lessons are learned; until at last he realizes that his wisdom lies in refusing to purchase future pain by temporary pleasure. And then he begins to starve out the desires by refusal to feed them, while by dwelling on the pains that gratification brings he cuts at their root with the axe of knowledge, wrought out of experience. At this stage of evolution, all average men, all but the lowest and roost brutish, have reached the stage when the voice of conscience is heard, and should therefore begin to consciously co-operate with the upward tendency out of the mire of materiality into the spiritual life.

How then can we break our bonds? The real answer is suggested in that law which I have been showing to you. The bonds are broken by these inevitable experiences which, life after life, teach the Soul the nature of the universe into which it has come. But desire is a binding force, and as long as there is desire so long must men come back to birth. The desire for good will draw it back as well as the desire for evil, the desire for religious happiness will draw it back as well as the desire for earthly joys; the desire for the praise of men, for love, for knowledge even. A Soul may desire results of a high and noble character still there is a desire for results, and this must bind him to places where the results are to be found. Therefore in order to get rid of karma we must get rid of desire. Not cease from action — that is unnecessary — but act without desire making every effort which is necessary, yet indifferent to the result. This is the familiar lesson given by Sri Krishna, this the essence of all truth. It is renunciation of desire, not of action, which makes the real Sannyasi, which makes the Renunciator, which makes the Yogi a *real* Yogi — not one only in the wearing of yellow garments and ashes, but a Yogī who has broken all the bonds of desire, and not simply one who is an outward renunciator. For the man of action who performs every action because it is his duty, and remains indifferent to the fruits thereof, that man in the world is the servant of God; he is one who performs every action, not for what it brings him but because it fills up something lacking which ought to be done in the world in which he lives as an agent of God. A man who realizes that the wheel of life must turn, and who takes part in the turning of the wheel — not for what the turning of the wheel may bring to him, but in order that the divine Life may circle in its course — he plays his part in working without attachment, without desire, and turns the wheel whether it brings him pleasure or pain, whether it brings him praise or blame, fame or ignominy, divine knowledge or ignorance — anything the wheel may bring him. He only perceives that it is his duty to co-operate with God while manifestation persists, and he therefore identifies himself with the God from whom the turning of the wheel proceeds. He is then one with Sri Krishna who declared that He had nothing to obtain in heaven or on earth, but that if He stopped acting, all would stop. And therefore the devotee who acts, not in order that he may get anything but in order that the divine purpose may be fulfilled, he works by way of sacrifice, he offers all his actions as sacrifices to God and remains indifferent to the fruits of the sacrifice, for they lie at the feet of God and not in the heart of the devotee. Such a man makes no karma, for such a man has no desire; such a man creates no links which bind him to earth, such a man is spiritually free, although around, him actions may spring up on every side. Thus is it when a man is born into the sphere of knowledge; thus is it when a man is born into the sphere of devotion; and the life of such a man is as an altar, and burning upon that altar is the flame of devotion and of knowledge. Every action is cast into the fire and is consumed therein, rising up as the smoke of a sacrifice, and leaving behind on the altar nothing save the fuel of knowledge and the fire of love.

Such then imperfectly sketched — for the subject is too vast — are the lines along which you may study the ancient problem, and which may make more clear to you the reason why pain and imperfection exist. We have seen that evil originates in limitation; we have seen that evil is but a relative thing, and how what we call evil is often only a veil of evil and beneath it a future good, we have seen how actions of men, when they are developed, become evil, which in a lower organization would not at all be evil; how as man proceeds onward and onward, he can use evil for his own perfecting; how man tries to escape from pain and to pursue pleasure: how desire remains in his heart, and brings him back to earth; how he goes forward and forward, purifying desire, identifying himself with the divine Actor in the universe; then how no further actions have binding force upon him; how such a man is free from evil, and free from all those bonds which tie the Souls of men; and finally how he becomes an altar from which the smoke of sacrifice goes up continually to the Eternal.

This indeed the life which alone is worth the living; this indeed the road along which lie peace and calm. This is realized by the true Yogī alone. Compare this with the life of the man who clings to the world, full of dissatisfaction, full of discontent. Look at the men and women around you; look at their faces; see how they are full of anxiety and of desire, of trouble and injustice; and see how men's hearts are pierced by pain and laid desolate by catastrophes, by miseries, by hopes and by fears; how they are tossed about and flung from side to side, and too often brought to ruin!

And then realize that Brahman is bliss. Bliss, but how? Bliss, because there is unity; bliss, because there is an absence of desire; bliss, because there is knowledge of permanence, which nothing that is transient can disturb. So shall the despairing human Soul find hope, if it is fixed on *Brahman;* so shall the disturbed human soul find peace. Who can deny *that* to the Soul that knows its source, that has found the Self? Thou art *Brahman.* There is nothing which can shake that; there is nothing which can undo that; there is nothing which can change that. It is fixed indissolubly upon the changeless, upon the Eternal Truth. It has nothing in it of earth, that it should ever pass away. The body is not the Soul; disease may mar it, accident may injure it, death may strike it away, but the Soul remains unchanged. The lower mind you may destroy, but there is no real loss; changed may be the individual circumstances, but the "I" is changeless. Separation between bodies may come, but the inner unity remains unbroken, and so any outer change must fail to drive to misery or to despair. Such a Soul stands as a rock in the midst of warring, surging billows. The waves of misfortune boil up around it, they may dash up against it, but only to be shattered into foam against its sides, and fall in snowy wreaths to decorate its base, and thus render it more beautiful than it was before. So is it with the Soul which identifies itself with the One; so is it with the Soul which by knowledge and devotion has removed everything which is fleeting, and has founded itself on that which is Divine. That is the goal; the goal which may be reached by you all, and the reaching of that goal is the *use of evil in the Universe*.

www.ingramcontent.com/pod-product-compliance
Lightning Source LLC
LaVergne TN
LVHW041503070426
835507LV00009B/794